SERENITY PATHWAYS
FAITH
FORGIVENESS
& *Moving*
FORWARD

TINNA BELLAMY

Copyright @ 2025 Tinna Bellamy
ISBN: 979-8-9986294-4-0
All rights reserved.

Author owns complete rights to this book and may be contacted in regards to distribution. Printed in the United States of America.

The copyright laws of the United States of America protect this book. No part of this publication may be stored electronically or otherwise transmitted in any form or by any means (electronic, photocopy, recording) without written permission of the author except as provided by USA copyright law. For permission requests, contact the author at the website below and/or through her social media handles.

Book Cover Design & Graphics: SHERO Publishing
Editing: Synergy Ed Consulting
Publishing: SHERO Publishing

SHEROPUBLISHING.COM

*"I didn't just survive—
I became."*

TINNA BELLAMY

TABLE OF CONTENTS

	Dedication	7
	Acknowledgements	8
	Introduction	10
CHAPTER 1	My Permanent Address	14
CHAPTER 2	Pieces of Her, Pieces of Me	22
CHAPTER 3	A Father in Theory	28
CHAPTER 4	Little Desk, Big Dreams	36
CHAPTER 5	Too Young to Know, Strong Enough to Do It Anyway	42
CHAPTER 6	Written in My DNA, Missing From My Life	54
CHAPTER 7	Degrees of Destiny	60
CHAPTER 8	Coming Home & Becoming Whole	68
CHAPTER 9	Becoming More Than I Survived	76
THE AUTHOR	Tinna Bellamy	84

SERENITY PATHWAYS

FAITH, FORGIVENESS & *Moving* FORWARD

TINNA BELLAMY

Dedication

To the little girl I used to be—
who learned how to survive in silence,
who found joy in small spaces,
and who never stopped believing there was more.
This is for you.

To my children—
your presence gave me purpose.
You are the reason I keep rising.
Thank you for choosing me.

To my grandmother—
your strength raised generations.
Your prayers covered us.
Your legacy lives on through me.

To every woman who's ever questioned her worth,
who's ever carried more than she should have,
and who's ever whispered "God, help me" through tears—
this is your reminder:
You can rise. You will heal. You are more.

And finally, to God—
the One who saw me, held me, and never let go.
Every page is proof of Your grace.

Acknowledgements

First and foremost, I give all honor and glory to God—the Author and Finisher of my faith. Without His grace, guidance, and unwavering love, this book and my journey would not be possible.

To my beloved grandparents, Roman and Irene Whitaker—thank you for the foundation of love, wisdom, and strength you laid for our family. Though you have gone on to be with the Lord, your legacy continues to inspire me every single day. I pray I've made you proud.

To my parents, Mary, Herman, and William—each of you has played a role in shaping the woman I am today. Through the lessons, the love, and even the challenges, I've become stronger, wiser, and more determined. I am forever grateful.

Ma, I love you and I appreciate you for being exactly who you are.

To my husband, Daniel—my rock and my greatest supporter for over 25 years—thank you for standing by my side through every high and every low. I thank God for creating you just for me. Your love, patience, and belief in me have made all the difference.

To my amazing daughters, Danyae and Taniya, and to my precious grandsons, Cohen and Kingston—you are my heart in human form. You are my greatest blessings. I thank God for choosing me as the vessel to bring you into this world. You inspire me daily to be the best version of myself.

I pray this journey serves as a testimony that faith, perseverance, and purpose can take you anywhere.

To my entire family and circle of friends—your encouragement, support, and love have been a constant source of strength. I cherish each of you more than words could ever express.

To my pastor, Dr. Jeffrey Chapman Sr., and Lady Sandie Chapman—thank you for your leadership, your wisdom, and your unwavering prayers. You have poured into my life in ways that words cannot fully capture. And to my Raleigh North Christian Center family—thank you for being a place of growth, faith, and community. Your support has been invaluable, and I'm honored to walk this journey alongside such a powerful body of believers.

To SHERO Publishing—thank you for bringing this vision to life and believing in the power of my story. Your dedication and expertise have made this process seamless and deeply rewarding.

To every reader and supporter who has purchased and read this book—*thank you*. Whether this story touches your heart, strengthens your faith, or helps you move forward in your own journey, know that it was written with you in mind.

And finally, once again, I give all glory, honor, and praise to God. Through Him, all things are possible. I pray His name is glorified on every page of this book and in every life it touches.

Introduction

Picture this: you're at a family gathering—the kind where there's more food than space on the table and more opinions than people. Your uncle is halfway through his usual monologue on why pineapple has no place on pizza (he's right, by the way—lol), and you've got something to say. But instead of speaking up, you stay quiet, nodding along, even though your inner voice is screaming, *"It's just fruit!"*

This story might seem trivial, but it's a microcosm of a larger problem: so many of us have opinions, thoughts, and ideas that never make it past the walls of our minds. Whether it's the fear of being wrong, the dread of confrontation, or just plain shyness, our voices often get trapped inside. But here's the good news—God didn't design us to be wallflowers in the garden of life. He gave us voices for a reason. As mentioned in Matthew 5: 14-16 (NIV), *"You are the light of the world. A town built on a hill cannot be hidden, neither do people light a lamp and put it under a bowl. Instead, they put it on a stand and it gives light to everyone in the house.* In the same way, let your light shine before others that they may see your good deeds and glorify your Father in heaven."

Our voices are more than just instruments for idle chatter. They are the tools we use to shape our world, to connect with others, and to declare who we are and what we stand for. Yet how often do we hesitate, holding back from speaking the truth that's burning inside us? Whether we're afraid of rejection, worried about causing waves, or just unsure if anyone's even listening, we let our voices be silenced far too often.

But imagine for a moment if everyone held back their thoughts. Where would we be if the dreamers, the leaders, the everyday people hadn't spoken up? History wasn't shaped by the quiet ones who hid in the shadows. It was shaped by those who dared to let their voices rise above.

SERENITY PATHWAYS
FAITH, FORGIVENESS & Moving FORWARD

TINNA BELLAMY

CHAPTER 1

My Permanent Address

Chapter 1
My Permanent Address

I was born in October of 1978, right around the time my grandparents moved into what would become our permanent address. I don't know if they moved in during August or September of that year, but before that, they lived in a downstairs apartment of a duplex. My mother and Aunt Arabell lived in the upstairs apartment.

Let me walk you through the family tree. My grandmother had seven children. Uncle Daniel was the oldest—she had him before she got married. When she married my grandfather, she left Uncle Daniel in the care of her mother and began her life with my grandfather. Together, they had six more children: Aunt Arabell, Aunt Lillie Bea, my mother Mary, Aunt Joyce, Uncle Roman Jr., and Aunt Irene. Interestingly, Aunt Arabell was named after my grandmother's youngest sister, and Aunt Lillie Bea was named after her oldest sister. That tells you just how deeply rooted in family my grandmother was. She didn't just name her children—she honored her lineage through them. She loved deeply and was determined to make sure her children were cared for.

Back to 1978—the year that feels like the true starting point of my life story. Aunt Arabell and my mom ended up sharing an apartment together—possibly the same one above my grandparents' duplex—until later that year when they both moved into the new home in Southern

Terrace, a subdivision in the town of Princeville. It wasn't just a move— it was a quiet homecoming to sacred soil. Princeville, the oldest town incorporated by freed slaves in the United States. It became the backdrop of our beginnings— where legacy whispered through the trees, and the strength of our ancestors rose up through the very ground we walked on.

That house, bought in 1978, was a modest three-bedroom, one-bathroom home, but it meant everything. My grandfather worked as a janitor at an elementary school in our town, and my grandmother worked at a local laundry facility. Together, they made it work, and they made that house a home for everyone. It was where people returned—especially during times of need.

Our family was tight-knit and raised to stick together no matter what. Aunt Joyce was still in high school when she gave birth, so my mom—who had dropped out by then—took care of both me and her son while Aunt Joyce went back to school. I once heard a story that my mom and Aunt Joyce had gotten into an argument, and my mom told her nephew, "I'm mad at your mama right now, but I still love you." That was how we operated—love stayed, even when tempers flared.

My grandmother was the glue. She raised her kids to support one another. They might bicker and fight, but no outsider was ever allowed to come between them. One minute they'd be arguing, the next they'd be laughing. That's what I saw growing up. Sometimes I wished I was raised with a sister, just so I could experience that strange but beautiful bond.

My cousins and I were raised more like siblings than first cousins. We all lived in the house together—Aunt Arabell and her three kids, my mom and her two kids, my Uncle Junior, and my grandmother. That house was full of life and noise, and it was home. I caught the school bus from there. I learned how to take care of others from there. And that sense of loyalty—of always having each other's backs—was ingrained in us by my grandmother.

She worked first shift, and my mom worked second shift. But I never remember feeling sad that my mom wasn't home in the evenings. During the day, before I started kindergarten, I spent time with her. I remember playing with Sesame Street cards and learning ABCs and numbers from materials my aunts brought home from preschool for my cousin. My mother may not have been affectionate, but I felt safe. She was simply like her mother—practical, not emotional.

Of course, there were times we got in trouble. I remember when one of my cousins broke a fan and didn't confess. For a week straight, we got spankings until the truth came out. Another time, we got whooped for pretending to be a drunken couple from the neighborhood. We were imitating them too well, and my aunt thought we had let them in the house.

I also remember when my brother Rodney was born in July of 1983. He was premature and had to stay in the hospital. I don't remember visiting him there, but I remember being at home when he finally arrived. At the time, we lived in Freedom Hill. My mom was recovering from a C-section, and Aunt Irene came to help her. One day, she brought food upstairs to my mom and said,

"Come on, Tinna, let's eat downstairs." I replied, "You brought her food, why can't you bring mine up here too?"

Once, after visiting my grandmother's house, we drove back home with my mom, baby brother, and me all in the front seat. My brother was crying nonstop. I reached over and put my hand over his mouth to quiet him. My mom snapped, "Don't you dare put your hand over his mouth!" I didn't say anything, but I thought, "Well, you tell him to be quiet, then!" Looking back, I was probably jealous. But I eventually got over it. I love my brother now, and I've even come to accept that he'll always be my mama's favorite.

My mom had a lot of male friends who came and went. Some weren't even single. I got in trouble once for telling my cousin about a man at the house. My cousin told his mom, who told mine, and the whole thing blew up. My mom fussed at me for "telling her business." My aunt clapped back, saying she shouldn't have had those men there in the first place. I learned not to repeat what I saw. I learned to carry secrets that weren't mine.

Today, as a mother and grandmother, I know I would never put that kind of pressure on a child. But back then, I was just trying to figure it all out. I didn't fully understand what was happening—I just knew how to keep my mouth shut.

My grandmother's spirit was strong—strict, yes—but full of purpose. She didn't play about education. Maybe it was because she only had a sixth-grade education, and my grandfather never finished high school either, but she was serious about school. I remember once, in second grade, I got a B on my report card and cried hard. She comforted me and said, "Just do better next time." But when I got a C in the fourth grade, after eating some cake from a neighbor down the street, she blamed it on that. "They jealous of you, and you shouldn't have eaten that cake," she said. She had a way of turning even small moments into lessons.

She was also very protective—borderline overprotective. We couldn't eat at other people's houses, and she had to personally know wherever we went. I remember in middle school, I was supposed to go to a Halloween party at the mall. My friend's mom was coming to pick me up, and I had told her I was going. But my Aunt Joyce told my grandma I shouldn't go, and that was that. My grandma wouldn't even let me answer the door to say I wasn't coming. To make things worse, Aunt Joyce ended up taking the other kids out, and I was furious. I didn't talk to her for a day.

Another time, also in seventh grade, I told my grandmother, and Aunt Irene I was going to run away. My aunt told me to go ahead. I walked out the driveway, only for my grandmother to yell, "Get your a** back in this house!" I came back in, of course—because where was I really going to go?

That house was the center of everything. Every Thanksgiving, Christmas, Sunday dinner—we were there. And even when we weren't celebrating anything, we were still at Grandma's house. It was the default setting of our lives. One of my grandmother's nieces told me she used to try to come pick us up sometimes, but my grandma didn't allow it. She was determined to raise us herself, to keep us close.

Looking back now as an adult, I realize my grandmother didn't really have a life outside her kids and grandkids. She poured everything into us. She made three meals a day, did laundry daily, hung clothes out on the line, and even tended to a garden. I used to help her plant seeds and read the almanac. She wasn't outwardly affectionate—she didn't say "I love you"—but she showed it in her own way.

She made sure we were warm at night, locked the doors, and checked in on us. I remember after I got baptized at church, I ran up to her for a hug. She didn't reject me, but she didn't hug me either. "Come on," she said. "Let's get you out of those wet clothes." That was love in her language. Practical. Protective. Constant.

My grandmother's dedication to her family showed us the wisdom of a woman who built up her family with love and sacrifice. As it says in Isaiah 46:4, "Even to your old age and gray hairs I am he, I am he who will sustain you. I have made you and I will carry you; I will sustain you and I will rescue you."

Just as God never stops caring for His children, my grandmother never stopped caring for hers. Her devotion was not just an act of duty, but a testament to the depth of her love—a legacy of selflessness and grace that shaped who we are today.

CHAPTER 1

PATHWAY POINTS
FAITH-FILLED INSIGHTS TO MOVE YOU FORWARD

1. Family is the First Foundation
Your roots matter. Even when life begins in chaos, the presence of one steady figure—like a grandmother, aunt, or mentor—can anchor you. Never underestimate the power of showing up consistently in someone's life.

2. Love Doesn't Always Look Like a Hug
Love isn't always expressed in words or warm gestures. Sometimes it looks like a hot meal, a locked door, or someone yelling, "Get your tail back in this house!" Learn to see love in its many forms—and give grace to those who show it differently.

3. Legacy is Built in the Small Moments
The routines, meals, and family traditions are more than chores—they're legacy-building. Even when your beginnings feel modest, the values passed down can shape your destiny. Honor your beginnings, even if they weren't perfect.

4. Childhood Lessons Become Adult Wisdom
The discipline, the routines, the chaos—they all become teachers. Don't dismiss what your younger self survived. Your childhood might have introduced struggle, but it also introduced strength.

5. Home is Where You Were First Seen
Whether it was a grandparent's kitchen, a crowded bedroom, or the school bus stop—those early places that saw your dreams and pain matter. Return to them not to stay, but to remember how far you've come.

CHAPTER 2

Pieces of Her, Pieces of Me

Chapter 2
Pieces of Her, Pieces of Me

My relationship with my mother is one of the most complex and tender parts of my story. She was my foundation, my first love, and also the first person I learned could let me down. I believe she loved me deeply, even when she was struggling to love herself. I now understand that her decisions weren't always about me—they were reflections of the battles she was silently fighting. But as a child, I only knew the impact, not the reasons.

I don't have a clear memory of when my mother started using drugs. I was still in elementary school, and to be honest, I think I blocked a lot of it out. What I do remember are the signs. We lived in Pioneer Court at the time, which many didn't call "the projects," but let me tell you—they were the projects. I was outside one day, and a boy in the neighborhood showed me something in his hand. It was a rock, and he said my mama told him she had one of those. I didn't understand then that it was crack, I didn't even remember asking what it was. Maybe I didn't want to know. Maybe it was easier to pretend.

Living with my mother during that time meant a lot of goodbyes to "normal." I remember the sounds of gunshots one early morning while my cousin Danielle was visiting overnight with us. We both woke up to the noise, but I told her to just go back to sleep. That was life in Pioneer Court. Things that would shake most people became background noise to us. We didn't have the luxury of panic.

And when I think of those moments of weakness, I'm reminded of Romans 8:28 that echoes the sentiment: *"And we know that all things work together for good to them that love God, to them who are the called according to his purpose."* Even in brokenness, there is purpose. My mother's life was complicated, but somehow, it was all part of a greater plan.

To answer questions from earlier reflections: What was she like before addiction? Were there special moments we shared? I honestly don't remember. How did her addiction progress over time? I don't know—I blocked a lot of it out. Did I ever confront her? Not really. I never pulled her aside to express my pain. The only time I really said anything was when she took my car and left drugs in it. And even then, I didn't go in on her the way I probably could have.

How do I feel now about my mother's legacy? It's still complicated. My mother is no longer using drugs, but she still has tendencies to use me—to ask for things, to take without always considering the cost to me. Still, the Word says we are to honor our mother and father, so I do what I can. I celebrate her birthdays, Mother's Day, Christmas. I take her to doctor's appointments. I also sometimes have paid a bill or two for her. I even dream of buying her a house one day—just because she is my mother.

But it's complicated.

A couple of years ago, I buried the mother I had in my mind. I was listening to a podcast about mother wounds, and it said, "You have to bury the mother you think you should have had." So, I did. And I've learned to accept the mother I actually have. I know she's done the best she could with what she had.

I've forgiven her. Just like I've forgiven my dad, but we will get to that later.

I believe both my parents did the best they could with what they were exposed to. Exposure leads to expansion. Sometimes people can only live by what they've seen. And when you haven't seen better, it's hard to be better.

What did I learn from all of this? If you're a parent struggling with addiction, please seek help—not just for yourself, but for your children. And if you're a child growing up with a parent in addiction, know that it's not your fault. Their choices aren't your burden. You are valuable, loved, and chosen.

Your worth is not defined by someone else's decision to stay or leave. Pain can be a catalyst for growth. Turn your pain into purpose. Your past doesn't define you—it can shape you, refine you, and even elevate you.

Forgiveness frees you. Forgiveness doesn't excuse the hurt. It just releases the hold that hurt has on you.

Build a support system. Family doesn't always mean blood. Mentors, friends, spiritual leaders—lean on the people who lift you up.

And most importantly—break the cycle. My brother, my cousins, and I have all done that. We're married, raising our children in stable homes. We've said, "It ends with us."

Your beginning may not have been perfect. But with God, your ending can be glorious. You do not have to carry shame or guilt from your past. The moment you repent and trust in Jesus, your slate is wiped clean. Let what you know in your head drop into your heart.

No matter what has happened, your future is bright. You are the only one who can stop you from becoming all God has purposed you to be. Don't let other people's limitations keep you from living in your calling.

Do you. Grow. Heal. Rise. Because you're worth it.

CHAPTER 2

PATHWAY POINTS
FAITH-FILLED INSIGHTS TO MOVE YOU FORWARD

1. Love Can Be Imperfect and Still Be Real
Just because love wasn't expressed the way you needed, doesn't mean it wasn't there. Some people love with limitations, and recognizing that can bring healing—not excuses, but understanding.

2. You Can Accept Without Agreeing
Forgiveness doesn't require approval. You can accept someone for who they are while acknowledging the pain they've caused. Letting go doesn't mean forgetting—it means choosing peace over bitterness.

3. Let Go of the "Mother You Wanted"
One of the hardest but most freeing steps is releasing the version of a parent you hoped for. Accepting the reality makes space for you to love them—and yourself—without unrealistic expectations.

4. Survival Often Starts with Silence
Learning to "keep your mouth shut" was survival. But healing comes when you learn to speak, process, and release what you once held in. Your story matters. Your voice is sacred.

5. Generational Pain Can Birth Generational Change
Your mother's struggles do not define your future. You have the power to break cycles and choose a different path. Her wounds may have shaped your beginning—but your choices will shape your legacy.

CHAPTER 3

A Father In Theory

Chapter 3
A Father in Theory

My father's name is Herman. I knew him, but I didn't know him—not in the way a child longs to know their dad. He wasn't a steady presence in my life. I saw him every couple of months, maybe. He would come around, say hello, maybe take me for a ride in his car. But he never stayed long, and I never stayed with him overnight. I never even stepped foot in his home.

There were times when he would take me riding around town—while he visited other people. We might have spent an hour or two together, tops. But I cherished even that small window of time, because it meant he thought of me. At least I hoped he did.

When I think back, I realize I had feelings about his absence that I didn't know how to name. I didn't cry over him. I didn't yell or ask why he wasn't there. I just quietly noticed. I noticed how he seemed to do more for his other children. My aunt introduced me to a brother once, at a shopping center. But my father never did the introductions himself. That kind of exclusion stays with a child. It teaches you that you are "other," even when no one says it out loud.

Still, in a strange way, I sometimes felt like I had the best of the worst. Compared to many of my cousins, my dad was more involved. He came around, and he paid child support. That was more than some of them could say. We even joked about it—saying I had the "best worst daddy" of the group. It was a sad joke, but it helped make sense of the imbalance.

There's one moment with him that still stands out. I got suspended from school in seventh grade for fighting. It was over a boy, of course. My mom made me tell my dad what happened. "Tell your daddy what you did," she said. So, I told him I got suspended. He looked at me and said, "Mm." That was it. No lecture. No punishment. Just a shrug and a smirk. It made me laugh a little—but it also made me feel unseen.

Even when people—including your parents—may not acknowledge your emotions or actions, God sees and knows us completely.

It's odd how you can crave someone's attention and resent them at the same time. I didn't expect much from him, so I didn't ask for much. Maybe that was a coping mechanism. Maybe that was survival. But the truth is—I wanted him to show up more. To care more. To claim me out loud.

And still, part of me believes he loved me the best way he knew how. He didn't have the tools to be the father I needed. Maybe he didn't know how to love past his own limitations. I don't say that to excuse him, but to understand him. There's a difference.

Herman has a very strong presence. Though he wasn't in the military, he carried himself like he was—disciplined, proud, and serious. He tried to be funny, but he wasn't. He was known as a ladies' man.

There were no birthday cards. No letters. No heartfelt moments. But he did buy me a car. I was on his health insurance. So, like I said, he did provide—just not emotionally. He wasn't there in the way I needed, but he did what he could from a distance.

Did that shape my trust issues? Absolutely. I don't know if it was because of my mother stealing from me at times, or because of my father not pouring into me like he should. But it all left an imprint, and I always wondered why. Thankfully, I married young—at twenty. I didn't spend my adult life dating. But even as a teenager, I always had a boyfriend or some male presence. I don't know if that was about filling a void left by my father, but it's something I've thought about.

Herman and I talk from time to time. Our conversations are light– never too deep, never too far beneath the surface. I've never told him what I really thought, never opened the door to the questions that kept me up at night. He's never apologized for the silence, for the absence I felt even when he was in the room. And I doubt he ever will. He didn't have to show up in the ways he did–but he did. Even if there were doubts–his or mine–he still took responsibility. He wasn't perfect. But he was present in the way he knew how. And that means something. It always will.

Growing up with an absent parent can be very challenging, but it can also shape you into a stronger, wiser, and more resilient person. I think we need to know that our worth is not defined by their absence.

And break the cycle. That's what I've tried to do. My mother was a single parent, but I've worked hard to change that narrative. Just because our fathers weren't in the house doesn't mean history has to repeat itself. I'm all about breaking generational curses and creating a new legacy.

God is the ultimate Father.

"Yet you, Lord, are our Father. We are the clay, you are the potter; we are all the work of your hand." – Isaiah 64:8 (NIV)

No earthly absence can replace the presence of God. He is always with you, shaping and molding you into something beautiful.

Love yourself, even when others didn't show you how.

Even if you didn't receive the love you wanted from a parent, you are still worthy of love—starting with how you treat yourself.

You may not have had a good beginning in life, but that doesn't mean you can't have a great finish. Whatever your past life was like, with Jesus, you can make a completely new start and have a bright future. Don't go through life burdened by guilt or shame from past relationships or failures. The moment you repent and put your faith in

Jesus, your sins are wiped away. Let what you know in your head drop to your heart.

That's what I want people to know: no matter what has happened in your past, your future can be as bright as you want it to be. You just have to be intentional. You are the only person who can stop you from becoming who God made and purposed you to be. So, keep going. Don't let outside forces or opinions stop you.

Do you. And let God handle the rest.

CHAPTER 3

PATHWAY POINTS
FAITH-FILLED INSIGHTS TO MOVE YOU FORWARD

1. You Can Grieve the Absence Without Resentment
Missing a parent who was physically present but emotionally absent is a valid form of grief. It's okay to mourn what you didn't receive—just don't let that mourning turn into bitterness.

2. Financial Support Can't Replace Emotional Presence
A check can't heal a wound. Children need more than provision—they need connection, conversation, and care. Absence wrapped in support still leaves a void.

3. Honor Isn't the Same as Approval
Honoring a parent doesn't mean ignoring their flaws. It means choosing grace over grudges and recognizing that respect can coexist with healthy boundaries.

4. Identity Is Rooted in Truth, Not Titles
Discovering the truth about your biological roots can be painful, but your identity is not limited to DNA. God has always known who you are—and His plan for your life is still intact.

5. What They Couldn't Give You, God Can
When earthly fathers fall short, your Heavenly Father steps in. His love is complete, unwavering, and healing. As Psalm 27:10 reminds us: *"Though my father and mother forsake me, the Lord will receive me."*

*"I learned early that sometimes the people you need the most won't be there—
but God always is, steady and unchanging."*

TINNA BELLAMY

CHAPTER 4

Little Desk, Big Dreams

Chapter 4
Little Desk, Big Dreams

The front porch taught me more about survival than safety. One day, I sat beside my mother on the front porch of our apartment in Pioneer Court when a woman stormed up, eyes wild, demanding to know if my mama had slept with her husband. Without flinching, my mama looked the lady in the eye as she continued to sit, ready for whatever came next. "No," she said coolly, pointing down the block. "His girlfriend lives down the street." Moments later, fists were flying three houses away, and I just sat there–watching, wondering, and shrinking. It wasn't the first time drama showed up uninvited, and it wouldn't be the last. Situations like that were regular guests in our world. That's why elementary school felt like holy ground.

Elementary school was a place where I found safety, even when everything outside the classroom felt uncertain. It was the one space where I could excel—where I felt seen, not because of who my family was or wasn't, but because of who I was. And for a little girl growing up in the projects with a mother battling addiction and a father who showed up when it was convenient, that mattered more than I can explain.

I was always smart. Gifted, really. I stayed on the A/B honor roll from the beginning. In fact, I remember being devastated in second grade when I got my very first B. I cried real tears over that grade. I wasn't just trying to get good grades for the sake of it—I wanted to prove I could be more than my environment. School gave me something I could control.

I absolutely adored my teachers. My kindergarten teachers, Ms. Hilliard and Mrs. Westry, were warm, strong Black women who made me feel like I belonged. I still smile when I think of them. In second grade, I had Ms. Batchelor and Ms. Whitehurst. They were both equally encouraging, always pushing us to strive for more. All of my teachers were Black women, and now that I'm older, I realize how powerful that was. They saw me. They understood me. And they taught me more than just reading and math—they taught me resilience.

But, even in a place where I thrived, I carried the weight of what was happening at home.

Even with all that was happening at home, school remained my place of peace. I earned awards, certificates, recognition. I caught the bus from my grandma's house most mornings, especially when my mom worked second shift. When I was at Princeville Elementary, I even walked home from school sometimes. And when I went to Bridgers in third grade, my Aunt Joyce would drop my cousin and me off to school, and then we'd walk back to her house after school until my mama got off work.

Looking back, I can't remember the lights ever being off or the water being cut. Somehow, my mama managed to keep the essentials on. But I also remember wanting more—wanting stability, wanting normalcy, wanting someone to notice when I was silently hurting. I didn't have the words to ask for help. I just kept smiling, kept studying, kept pretending everything was fine.

My favorite subject in school was math. I remember being in a spelling bee in third grade. I won the class round but missed the very first word in the school-wide competition. I'll never forget how that word is spelled now. Even in that moment of disappointment, I held onto my desire to be great.

I wanted to be a doctor when I grew up—an OB-GYN, specifically—because of the Cosby Show. I wanted to help people. I had the grades. I had the dreams. But somewhere along the way, I got tired. Life was heavy. My grandmother wanted me to become a nurse. But back then, I thought being a nurse wasn't good enough—I believed doctors were the best of the best. Now I know better. Nurses are the backbone. They're the ones by the bedside, doing the hands-on care. My daughter is now studying to become a nurse, and I have so much respect for the profession. But at the time, I had tunnel vision: I wanted to be the best, and in my mind, that meant being a doctor.

I ended up going to college and majoring in psychology. I was still determined to have "Dr." in front of my name. I didn't get there in the traditional way, but I'm not done. I still plan to go to graduate school—because that dream, that title, still matters to me.

When I think about the lessons of my childhood, one scripture stands out: *"I know what it is to be in need, and I know what it is to have plenty. I have learned the secret of being content in any and every situation, whether well-fed or hungry, whether living in plenty or in want. I can do all this through him who gives me strength."* – Philippians 4:12-13 (NIV)

There are times when we walk through seasons of lack, but that verse reminds me that strength and endurance come from God, no matter the circumstances.

Obstacles will come. That's life. But we must not let those obstacles stop us. No matter what you've been through, you are destined for greatness. Keep striving, keep believing, and keep walking in your purpose.

The race isn't given to the swift but to the one who endures to the end. Sometimes you're running. Sometimes you're crawling. Sometimes you're moving at a snail's pace. But keep moving. Because the moment you stop moving—that's when you stop living.

I think back to the movie *Finding Nemo*, when Dory said, "Just keep swimming. Just keep swimming." That's what we have to do in life. We keep pushing. We keep swimming. We keep going to fulfill the purpose God has placed within us.

And that's what I've learned: no matter where you start, no matter how shaky the ground feels beneath you—keep moving.

CHAPTER 4

PATHWAY POINTS
FAITH-FILLED INSIGHTS TO MOVE YOU FORWARD

1. Your Environment Doesn't Define Your Potential
Even if you grow up in the midst of struggle, you can still rise. You can find excellence, purpose, and peace—even in the projects. God plants greatness in unlikely places.

2. Excellence is a Form of Resistance
Pursuing good grades, dreaming big, and setting goals can be powerful ways to break cycles. Your effort is not just about achievement—it's a declaration that your story will be different.

3. Love is Shown in Many Languages
Affection isn't always verbal or physical. Sometimes love shows up in meals cooked, bus rides coordinated, or school shoes cleaned. Learn to see the love—even if it doesn't come wrapped the way you expected.

4. Resilience is Built in the Small Moments
It's not always the big tragedies that shape us—it's the everyday choices to keep showing up, keep trying, and keep believing. Every spelling bee, every bedtime prayer, every "do better next time" adds up.

5. You Are Not What You Wear or What You Lack
God's favor isn't based on name brands or new shoes. What you carry in your heart is more powerful than what's on your back. Never let your appearance convince you that you're any less valuable.

CHAPTER 5

Too Young To Know, Strong Enough To Do It Anyway

Chapter 5
Too Young to Know, Strong Enough to Do It Anyway

Middle School

Middle school was the beginning of both awakening and weariness for me. It was the space between childhood and adolescence where I started noticing not just what was happening around me, but also what was missing. It was the time when I began to understand the weight of my mother's addiction, the distance of my father, and the truth that I had to become my own advocate.

Seventh grade marked the first time I stepped into a new school year without the usual small joys—no fresh press, no new shoes, no new outfit. Normally, I'd have at least a straightened hairstyle and something new to wear, even if it wasn't expensive. But that year, nothing. My hair wasn't done. My clothes weren't new. And I didn't realize at the time that it had everything to do with my mother's drug use. All I knew was she said she didn't have the money, and that was that.

Despite how I showed up on the outside, I was still smart—very smart. Academically, I thrived. I earned recognition and awards. But socially, I struggled. The girls didn't like me, and I never really knew why. Maybe it was because the boys did like me. Maybe it was because I was confident in class. Whatever it was, it made me a target. I was constantly picked on, and fights became almost expected.

Still, I was driven. At the end of that same school year, I received multiple academic awards—more than most. I had become an expert at carrying chaos in one hand and excellence in the other. I didn't have a choice. Excelling in school became my escape hatch, my one-way ticket out of instability.

I also became more self-reliant. I stopped asking for help. I had written to my Aunt Irene before when I needed something, and sometimes she helped—giving me hand-me-down clothes or picking me up small things. She didn't have kids, and neither did my Aunt Bea, so they'd do what they could, especially around Christmas. But I never wanted to ask too much. I knew they were my aunts—not my mother. And I never wanted to be a burden.

That habit of not asking for help stuck with me. Even now, it's hard for me to reach out. I think it traces back to that deep feeling of not being able to depend on the people who were supposed to be there. My parents were absent in different ways, and that absence forced me to grow up faster than I should have.

High School

By high school, the challenges deepened. I entered those years with the same academic drive, but the weight of everything I was carrying became heavier. My mother was still struggling with addiction. My father was a ghost. I was trying to be a "normal" teenage girl—thinking about school dances, friendships, and my future—while holding everything together at home.

The Upward Bound Excel program gave me a glimpse of something better. My tenth-grade summer at Clark Atlanta University changed my life. For six weeks, I was surrounded by possibility. The experience was like a breath of fresh air. For the first time, I could imagine my life beyond the limitations of my hometown. I was surrounded by other bright students, mentors, and a vision of what life could look like if I just kept pushing. I fell in love with learning all over again. That summer gave me hope, and I held onto it tightly.

So, when they planned a reunion my senior year, I was beyond excited. I was looking forward to seeing friends from the program. Returning to that space where I felt free, and reminding myself of the life I was striving for. But that reunion never happened for me– at least not the way I planned. A few days before the reunion, my mother took my car—the Ford Escort my father had bought me, and even though it wasn't fancy, it was mine. Without asking. Without warning. She was gone for two, maybe three days.

I needed to get my hair done. I had it all planned. But with no car, there was no hair appointment, therefore, no reunion. When she returned, it was too late. I opened the door and saw her drugs sitting in the car. I didn't scream, but I raged on the inside. It felt like a punch in the gut. I didn't say anything at first. I just stared. And then the anger came– raging, quiet, deep. I didn't curse her–not out loud, but the things I said in my head, the way I screamed silently, and wishing she was dead silently, I will never forget. I told Aunt Joyce, but she was living her own life, raising her child, and dealing with her own challenges. My grandmother, who had always been a rock, didn't drive and was a dialysis patient by that time. Everyone had their own storms. And me? I just weathered mine alone, nobody stepped in. No one saved the day. And honestly, I didn't ask. I had longed stopped expecting people to come through for me, at least in the way I needed and expected for them to be.

That was the hardest part. Not just missing the trip, but the confirmation that I had to take care of myself. I began carrying the emotional load of being my own protector and my own motivator. I didn't always get it right, but I kept going. And I kept believing–believing that somehow, someway, I made it through.

Daniel—my husband now—was my boyfriend then. We met when I was a cashier at Food Lion, and he worked in produce. I was taking my grandmother grocery shopping when he sent a coworker to ask for my number. I told that coworker, "If Daniel wants my number, he better come ask himself." He did, and we talked on the phone for hours that night.

He took me to my senior prom. He asked me to be his girlfriend at the hospital when I was visiting my grandmother. We stayed close, even after he went to NC State, and I went off to college.

High school was a contradiction. I was present but invisible. Surrounded but alone. Ambitious but unsupported. I had a car but no direction. A family but no safety net. Still, I made it. Every grade. Every test. Every award. I was still standing. **Then came college.**

College Years

College was never just about getting a degree for me. It was about becoming someone different than what life had tried to hand me. I didn't have parents dropping me off with care packages and proud tears. I had grit. Hunger. And a deep belief that I was meant for more.

I went off to North Carolina A&T and it felt like freedom—but it was also lonely. I was still figuring out how to ask for help. Then, in the middle of all that growth and newness, I found out I was pregnant.

My birthday is in October, I had just turned 19. I wasn't feeling well around homecoming. I missed the entire celebration. I told my best friend, Jessuita I didn't feel right, and eventually took a pregnancy test.

I cried when I saw the result. This wasn't how my life was supposed to go. I told Daniel. He said, "It's going to be okay." And I told my Aunt Irene next. She helped schedule a doctor's appointment and told me, "You have options. Whatever you decide, we're here."

I decided to keep the baby.

At the time, I didn't believe in abortions. My views have evolved since then, and I now support a woman's right to choose. Still, I was terrified–overwhelmed by shame, fear, and the weight of everything. I thought I was about to lose. One night, in a moment of desperation, I tried to fall down the cement stairs of my dorm, hoping it would end the pregnancy without me having to make the choice. I didn't fall. And after a few weeks, I realized that even though I was scared, part of me already loved the life growing inside me. I was broken, but something in me wanted to protect what hadn't even been born yet.

When I went home for Thanksgiving, I told my mom and grandma. My grandmother was disappointed. She didn't want me to have the baby. She wanted me to finish school. She said, "That boy is getting his education. You need to get yours."

I told her I would. I promised I wouldn't drop out. And I meant it. She didn't talk to me much during that break. She was cold, distant. But I understood.

Daniel proposed to me on Mother's Day. After that, her heart softened. Once her heart softened, she suggested that she and my Aunt Joyce could take care of the baby while I went back to school. I told her, I didn't want to give up my baby. I confidently said to her, "I made my bed hard, I had to lay it." I didn't want my baby calling anyone "Mommy," but me. When the baby was born in July, she was in love. She held the baby, doted on her. She even sent my brother Rodney to Greensboro to help me after delivery. My mama stopped using drugs when my baby was born. Maybe it was the innocence of a new life, or maybe it was the silent understanding that I wouldn't let history repeat itself. Whatever it was, my baby saved us both in her own way.

I tried to go back to school that August. But I think I had postpartum depression. I was juggling school, work, and motherhood. Some of my family and my closest friends helped watch the baby. Daniel came every weekend. But I was failing. Broke. Overwhelmed.

So, I dropped out. I got a full-time job. Daniel moved to Greensboro, and we got married in August 1999. Two years later, we welcomed our second child.

We struggled. We didn't manage our money well. At one point, Daniel stayed with his brother, and I stayed with my Aunt Joyce because we couldn't find a place to live. Eventually, Daniel's parents helped us get an apartment in their name. We moved to Angier.

I wasn't built to be a stay-at-home mom. I love my kids, but I needed something for me. In October, I got a job as a medical records director at the nursing home Daniel worked at. I felt like I had a piece of myself again; it was the beginning of my career in medical coding, a path I didn't even know would one day become the key to building the life I prayed for. That role gave me confidence, consistency, and a steady income that helped support my family.

Our family was growing. Our love was real. But there were still things I didn't know about myself—pieces of the puzzle missing.

And I was about to find one of the biggest missing pieces of them all.

CHAPTER 5

PATHWAY POINTS
FAITH-FILLED INSIGHTS TO MOVE YOU FORWARD

1. Your Pain Doesn't Cancel Your Purpose
Even when your story starts with rejection or absence, God can still use your life for impact. You were created with purpose, and no one else's decision—not even a parent's absence—can erase God's plans for you.

2. Forgiveness is the First Step to Freedom
Releasing bitterness doesn't excuse what happened, but it does unchain your heart. Forgiveness allows you to reclaim your power and walk forward without dragging the weight of the past.

3. Healing Begins With Acceptance
Sometimes, the greatest peace comes when you stop expecting people to become who they've never been. Accepting your parents as they are—without pretending or suppressing pain—creates space for healing and wholeness.

4. God Fills the Gaps Others Leave Behind
Psalm 27:10 reminds us that even if our mother or father forsake us, the Lord will receive us. Where people failed, God remains. He is a constant Father who never leaves, never fails, and always restores.

5. You Can Break the Cycle
Generational change starts with one decision. I chose to become the mother, wife, and woman my younger self needed—and so can you. *Legacy isn't what you inherit; it's what you build through intention, faith, and obedience.*

"Even when people fail you, God never will. His love is constant, His plans are perfect, and His purpose for your life is still unfolding."

TINNA BELLAMY

CHAPTER 6

Written in My DNA, Missing From My Life

Chapter 6
Written in My DNA, Missing From My Life

In September 2022, I went to the funeral of a family friend with my Aunt Joyce. At the time, my husband, children, and I were living in Angier, but we went back to Tarboro every weekend. Whenever something was happening back home, I was there spending time with family.

At the funeral, I saw a man I had seen before—William. I told my aunt, "Every time I see that man, he's always staring at me. I think he's a pervert." She looked at me and said, "You need to talk to your mother about that."

That evening, when my mother got off work, I told her what Joyce had said. For the first time in my life, my mother looked afraid. She hesitated. She stuttered. That wasn't like her—my mother was always a straight shooter. So I asked, "Is this man my dad?" And I told her, "You might as well tell me the truth. I'm married. I have kids. Just say it."

She admitted, "Yes, it's a possibility."

The next day, she took me by his house. She gave me his number and told me how to look him up in the phone book. That Monday, I called. He wasn't home, so I left a message. He called back. I told him, "My name is Tinna. My mother is Mary. She told me it's possible you're my father."

He didn't hesitate. He said, "Oh, okay," as if he'd been expecting the call. We agreed to meet that coming weekend in Tarboro. My husband, children, and I met him at Golden Corral. From the moment I saw him, it felt familiar. Safe. We clicked instantly.

He said, "We should do a DNA test to be sure." I agreed. I tested at a clinic in Fayetteville, and he tested in Tarboro. Six weeks later, the results came back: 99.999%. I opened the letter and cried.

I cried because I was mad. I cried because I was relieved. I cried because the man I thought was my father—Herman—wasn't. And all the anger I had carried toward him over the years suddenly felt misplaced.

But I also cried—because William was so kind, so open, so willing. He accepted me without hesitation. And so did his son, Donyell. When we visited his house, Donyell brought a cigar that read *"It's a girl."* He gave me flowers and balloons, and he even bought toys for my kids. His other son, Ronyell, invited me to his home the following weekend. It was overwhelming—but in the most healing way. Their love reminded me why I love so hard, why I give so much. That's just who I am. And that's who they were too.

That moment changed something in me. I didn't know I needed that acceptance so badly until I received it. My spirit felt seen. Understood.

I had always doubted. I remember telling my sister Tonya, Herman's daughter, "I don't look like y'all. I don't act like y'all." And she would say, "Girl, shut up. You're one of us."

But when I learned the truth, everything made sense. I needed to know. I needed the truth because I had lived in lies long enough—being the daughter of an addict who stole from me and being raised in uncertainty.

After the DNA confirmation, I called Herman. I took him to Golden Corral. I told him everything. He said he'd heard rumors that I might not be his. But he never looked into it. Neither did William, even though he knew there was a chance. When my mom got pregnant, she had called William, but my grandmother told her to hang up because he was married. She told her not to put a baby on a married man.

Regardless, William embraced me. His family did too. He introduced me to his siblings, nieces, nephews—and they welcomed me with open arms.

I also met with Herman's children to tell them the truth. Their response? "You're still our sister. That doesn't change."

DNA doesn't lie—but love doesn't either. I noticed I had some of William's traits too—like sensitive skin and eczema. Things started clicking. And spiritually, I grew.

I learned to trust my inner knowing. God speaks in stillness. I learned to ask the hard questions because the truth really does set you free. I learned to forgive silence, even when the silence hurt. I made room for redemption. Just because someone shows up late doesn't mean they can't still help change the ending.

William wasn't there in my childhood, but he became an incredible grandfather. He supported my kids—holidays, birthdays, graduations. He was present. He even taught them to drive before they were supposed to. He showed them what love looks like.

I thank God that my children didn't just see stability on their father's side. They saw healing on mine. They saw what was broken become whole. Meeting my father changed everything. It shifted my mindset. It grounded me. It allowed me to become the woman I am today.

And for that, I am grateful.

CHAPTER 6

PATHWAY POINTS
FAITH-FILLED INSIGHTS TO MOVE YOU FORWARD

1. Trust Your Inner Voice
If something in your spirit feels unsettled, don't ignore it. God often whispers truth through our intuition. For years, I felt like something didn't quite add up—and I was right. Listen to that still, small voice inside you. It might be leading you to healing.

2. Ask the Hard Questions
Even when the truth is uncomfortable, it's necessary. Asking my mom the question I'd avoided for decades changed my entire life. Sometimes the answers will shake you, but they'll also set you free.

3. Embrace Unexpected Love
Love can show up in surprising places. Meeting my biological father later in life reminded me that it's never too late for new beginnings. Be open to receiving love—even when it doesn't come the way you expected.

4. Leave Space for Forgiveness and Redemption
Forgiveness doesn't erase the pain, but it loosens its grip on your heart. I had to forgive both my parents—not just for what they did or didn't do, but for the versions of them I created in my head. Grace allowed me to release bitterness and embrace growth.

5. Redefine What Family Means
DNA connects us, but love defines us. Both my biological and legal fathers played roles in my life. And my children were blessed to witness healing, connection, and unconditional love. Don't let broken beginnings keep you from building a beautiful future.

FAITH, FORGIVENESS & MOVING FORWARD

CHAPTER 7

Degrees of Destiny

Chapter 7
Degrees of Destiny

Finding my dad was a critical moment in my life. It felt like it catapulted everything into motion. Around that time, my husband left the nursing home where he had been working in Dunn and got a job in telecommunication, doing business to business sales in the Raleigh area. Since he was commuting from Angier to Raleigh every day, we decided to move closer to the city.

I didn't want to move without securing a job first. I applied and landed a position in the medical records department at NC State. That experience in health information stuck with me—it felt like my calling. It also reminded me of the promise I made to my grandmother: that I would finish school. Although I had quit previously, this new job reignited my drive.

North Carolina A&T didn't offer a health information management degree, so I enrolled online at Edgecombe Community College and earned my associate degree. Sadly, my grandmother passed away on June 26, 2004, and never got to see me walk across the stage. But I worked hard. I finally graduated in 2008 with my degree in health information management.

My kids and I often did our homework together at the kitchen table. I would tell them the same things my grandmother told me—education is important. Stay in school, do your best, and never give up.

Eventually, I became certified as a Registered Health Information Technician (RHIT) and earned my Certified Coding Specialist (CCS) certification. Around that time, my husband, who was working at Wachovia, began learning about real estate through his clients—builders, contractors, and investors. Inspired, he brought that knowledge home. He's always had a sharp business mind and was full of ideas. He wanted to get into real estate, and I was right there with him, supporting every step.

In 2013, we purchased our first rental property. We had already bought our own home in 2005, so real estate investment became our next big step. Our daughter Danyae was planning to attend ECU, and we bought a condo in Greenville at Sterling Point. When she finally went off to school, she didn't want to live in Sterling Point, and honestly, I didn't want her there either. She ended up finding a better property in Rollins.

We bought that property too, and once she moved in, we rented out the other two rooms to college students. That meant her room and board were covered, and the mortgage was paid. She just had to handle utilities, which she did by working part-time. She probably got that work ethic from her mama!

By 2014, we had four rental properties, including the first house we ever lived in. That year, I made it a goal to buy two properties every year. We were focused on building generational wealth and establishing a legacy.

Danyae graduated from college in three years—ambitious just like her mom—and our youngest daughter Taniya wasn't happy about sharing her high school graduation spotlight. In 2019, Danyae bought her first home at the age of 20, with our guidance. Taniya, not to be outdone, purchased her first home at 19 in 2020.

Taniya moved into her property, continued school, and worked while renting out rooms to cover her mortgage. By then, we had instilled in both our daughters the value of building wealth and legacy. We knew land wasn't being made anymore, so we were determined to acquire as much as we could.

In 2021, Danyae purchased her second property after becoming pregnant with our grandson Cohen. And in Jesus' name, Taniya will be purchasing her second property soon after she graduates from nursing school. We've passed down more than houses—we've passed down vision.

I eventually returned to North Carolina A&T and earned my bachelor's degree in 2021. Then I went on to earn my master's degree in health administration. I kept my promise to my grandmother.

In 2020, we officially launched Bellamy Investment Group Properties, LLC. I became a broker-in-charge with four agents under me. We primarily help young people, especially those we know, get pre-qualified and purchase their first properties. We're passionate about helping others—especially our people—build wealth through real estate.

So, what would I say to someone reading this? Keep moving. Keep striving. Don't let life stop you. On the pathway to peace and purpose, there will be roadblocks and challenges. But chip away at them, pray through them, and knock down the walls you've built that keep you from progress.

Start where you are. Use what you have. Every class, every certification, every step is an investment in your future. Education isn't a detour—it's a doorway.

Don't be afraid to sharpen your skills at any stage. Your children are watching, and your example leads them forward. My degree wasn't just for me—it was a legacy move.

Faith without a blueprint is still faith. I didn't always know how things would work, but I moved anyway. When you take one step, God provides the next. Let's walk by faith and not by sight.

Build wealth with wisdom. Don't just buy homes—build legacy. Pass down what you learn. Teach your children to start ahead, not over.

Proverbs 24:3-4 says, "By wisdom a house is built, and through understanding it is established; through knowledge its rooms are filled with rare and beautiful treasures."

I'm building legacy through faith, knowledge, and perseverance. I'm creating abundance—not just for me, but for generations to come.

As I continue walking the pathway toward serenity—of faith, forgiveness, and moving forward—I remind you: don't stop. Keep walking. Keep believing. God holds the future, and with Him, all things work together for your good.

CHAPTER 7

PATHWAY POINTS
FAITH-FILLED INSIGHTS TO MOVE YOU FORWARD

1. Start Where You Are, Use What You Have
I didn't have it all figured out when I started. What I had was faith, determination, and a promise to my grandmother that I'd finish school. You don't need the perfect plan to move forward—you just need to begin.

2. Your Children Are Watching You Become
Going back to school and investing in myself wasn't just about me—it was about showing my children what's possible. Every degree, every property, every step forward was a blueprint for them to follow. Lead by becoming.

3. Build Legacy, Not Just Wealth
Real estate gave us more than money—it gave us purpose. We weren't just buying homes; we were building generational wealth. Teaching our children how to own and invest gave them a head start and us peace of mind.

4. Don't Let Setbacks Define the Finish Line
I quit school. I restarted. I pivoted. I climbed back up. Life doesn't move in a straight line—but every setback prepared me for the comeback. Stay the course and trust God's timing.

5. Walk Your Path with Faith and Intention
I've learned that every step, even the hard ones, leads somewhere meaningful. Keep praying, keep pushing, and chip away at whatever stands in your way. God doesn't ask us to see the whole staircase—just to take the next step.

*"I didn't have it all figured out, but I moved anyway—
one step at a time, trusting that God
would light the path as I walked."*

TINNA BELLAMY

CHAPTER 8

Coming Home & Becoming Whole

Chapter 8
Coming Home & Becoming Whole

Coming home is never just about geography. It's not just a change in address or a shift in scenery. Coming home, for me, means facing everything I once tried to outrun—the pain, the people, the memories... and most of all, myself.

After all the detours of college life, the early days of motherhood, and building a life with Daniel, I found myself visiting the very streets I used to dream of escaping. Driving through my old neighborhood stirred something deep—familiar and complicated. The same houses. The same streets. And yet, I was not the same girl who once walked them.

My grandmother passed in 2004, but the house where I spent so much of my childhood is still in the family. My mother lives there now. And when I visit, I'm reminded of everything that space holds—love, loss, survival, and strength. It's not just a building. It's a living archive of where I come from.

There's comfort in the familiar—the scent of something cooking in the kitchen, the creak of the front steps, the way the light hits the living room just right in the afternoon. But there's also a quiet tension, not from chaos, but from memory. I've changed, and so has my mother. She's no longer battling the addictions that once gripped our lives. That truth alone feels like a miracle.

I no longer arrive home hoping for something different—I arrive grateful for what is. My mother may not always have had the tools, but she has always had love. And now, in this season, I can see her with softer eyes. We've both survived things that tried to break us. And maybe, in our own ways, we're healing together.

Coming home means seeing the people who knew me before I knew myself. The aunts who helped raise me. The cousins who feel like siblings. The neighbors who never missed a thing. They remind me of who I've always been, and in some ways, who I will always be.

Still, I feel the difference. I don't belong to that version of life anymore. I visit, but I no longer live in that space—physically or emotionally. I'm no longer the girl trying to escape. I'm a woman who built something new. When I come home now, it's not to be rescued—it's to remember.

And remembering has been part of my healing. Because healing isn't always loud. Sometimes it looks like sitting in the same room where you once cried and feeling peace instead of pain. Sometimes it sounds like laughter where silence once lived. Sometimes it feels like walking through the door, not with fear, but with ease.

These days, when I visit, I carry deep gratitude—and deep relief. Gratitude for my roots. For the resilience and the rhythm of the place that made me. And relief that I didn't have to stay planted there. I can return and honor my beginning without being tied to it.

My family still treats me like I'm from where I'm from—and I love that. Because I am. No matter what I've accomplished, they see me. And that keeps me grounded in the best way. There's something sacred about being able to come home, honor it, love it, and leave with peace in your heart—knowing you made it out, and yet, never really left it behind.

For most of my life, I thought surviving was the goal. I thought waking up, getting through the day, and making it to the next without breaking down was strength. And it was—for a while. But there came a point where I had to decide that surviving wasn't enough. I wanted more. I deserved more. And I was becoming someone who believed that.

I had survived the silence of an absent father and the chaos of a mother lost in addiction. I had survived instability, abandonment, judgment, and quiet seasons of lack. I had survived the sting of rejection, the weight of responsibility too soon, and the ache of waiting for someone to show up who never did. But survival doesn't always mean healing. Survival keeps you alive—but healing teaches you how to live.

"He heals the brokenhearted and binds up their wounds." – Psalm 147:3

This scripture tells me that while survival keeps us moving, only God can heal our wounds. *"For I will restore health to you, and your wounds I will heal, declares the Lord…" –* Jeremiah 30:17. Survival isn't the end goal. God provides full restoration and healing.

I realized I had spent years defining myself by what I had been through. And while my story shaped me, it didn't have to own me. I was more than the daughter of a struggling mother. More than the "smart girl" who never had her hair done. More than the teen mom who almost didn't go back. I was more than the whispers, the pity, the assumptions. I had depth. I had dreams. And more importantly, I had something to give.

Becoming more than what I survived started with choice. I had to choose to stop rehearsing old pain. To stop measuring my worth by who didn't love me right or show up the way I needed. I had to forgive people who never apologized and let go of questions that would never be answered.

I started listening to the still, small voice within me—the one that had been trying to speak all along. The voice that said, "You are not what happened to you. You are who you choose to become." And I chose to become a woman of intention.

"Be not conformed to this world: but be ye transformed by the renewing of your mind..." – Romans 12:2

This verse powerfully reinforces the idea that you are not defined by what happens to you but by the choices you make to grow, transform, and walk in purpose.

I went back to school. I showed up for my children. I pushed past every limitation that had tried to box me in. And though the process wasn't perfect—and I wasn't perfect—I was present. I was progressing. And I was proud.

I started using my voice—not just to tell my story, but to inspire others to rise from theirs. I realized my pain had purpose. My mess carried a message. My survival had a sound—and I wasn't afraid to let it be heard anymore. I didn't just want to exist. I wanted to build, to thrive, to impact.

Becoming more than what I survived also meant confronting myself. I had to stop hiding behind strength and allow myself to feel. To grieve what I didn't get. To admit when I was hurting. To acknowledge that even the strongest woman needs somewhere soft to land.

I learned to surround myself with people who poured back into me—who didn't just want access to my strength but honored my story. I protected my peace. I reclaimed my time. I started building a life I didn't need a vacation from—one rooted in grace, purpose, and legacy.

I am not just a survivor. I am a cycle breaker. A builder. A woman becoming. And I've learned that true power comes not from pretending you've never been through anything—but from standing boldly and saying, "I'm still here. And I'm still rising."

My mindset is to continue to rise, continue to press forward, and continue to become all that God has called me to be.

CHAPTER 8

PATHWAY POINTS
FAITH-FILLED INSIGHTS TO MOVE YOU FORWARD

1. Growth and Grace Can Happen at the Same Time
You don't have to have it all figured out to move forward. God doesn't require perfection—He works with our progress. Even when life gets messy, grace shows up in the middle of it.

2. Your Detours Are Still Part of the Plan
Life may not look like the dream you first imagined—but every pause, pivot, and unexpected pregnancy can still serve a purpose. Romans 8:28 reminds us that *all things work together for good when we love Him and walk in our calling.*

3. Motherhood Doesn't Mean the End of Your Dreams
Having a child while still finding yourself is hard—but it's not a death sentence to your purpose. Like me, you can parent and pursue destiny. You may take the long route, but you can still finish the race.

4. You Don't Need Outside Validation to Be Enough
Whether people cheer for you or not, keep going. I found my strength by showing up—even when no one else could see the weight she was carrying. Remember: God sees. God knows. And God rewards faithfulness.

5. Real Love is Shown Through Action, Not Just Intention
Daniel's support during college, pregnancy, and postpartum showed that love isn't about saying the right thing—it's about showing up. Choose relationships that bring out your strength, support your goals, and help you rise.

*"No matter how many storms I face,
I know that with God's strength and my determination,
I will always find my way forward."*

TINNA BELLAMY

CHAPTER 9

Life Nuggets: Faith, Forgiveness & Moving Forward

Chapter 9
Life Nuggets: Faith, Forgiveness & Moving Forward

If there's one thing life has taught me, it's this: you can go through fire and still come out whole. Not untouched—but whole. Not the same—but stronger. My story isn't just a series of survival chapters. It's a testimony of grace, grit, and growth. And through it all, I've carried three unshakable truths: **faith, forgiveness, and moving forward.**

Faith

Faith kept me from losing my mind when I felt like everything around me was falling apart. It was my anchor when the ground beneath me kept shifting. It was my quiet "yes" to God even when I didn't have the words to pray out loud. Faith told me I was more than what I came from, and that there was purpose in my pain—even when I couldn't see it yet.

"You will keep in perfect peace those whose minds are steadfast, because they trust in you." Isaiah 26:3 (NIV)

" My grace is sufficient for you, for my power is made perfect in weakness. Therefore, I will boast all the more gladly about my weaknesses, so that Christ's power may rest on me."
2 Corinthians 12:9 (NIV)

I've learned that faith isn't always loud. Sometimes it's a whisper. A deep breath. A decision to show up when you'd rather stay in bed. Faith helped me raise my children when I was still growing up myself. It helped me believe in a better future when I had every reason to give up. It reminded me that the same God who carried me through my lowest moments had greater in store. And I believed Him.

Forgiveness

Forgiveness has been one of the hardest, most necessary parts of my journey. I had to forgive people who never said they were sorry. People who left me. People who disappointed me. I had to forgive my father for not being what I needed, my biological father for not fighting to know the truth about me and my mother for not being the mother that I wanted her to be. I even had to forgive family who meant well but missed the mark.

But the real work was forgiving *myself*—for all the times I accepted less than I deserved, for all the moments I stayed silent when I should have spoken up, for all the years I walked in shame instead of boldness.

Forgiveness didn't mean forgetting. It didn't mean I pretended the hurt never happened. It just meant I refused to let the past dictate my future. It meant I gave myself permission to be free.

Forward

I've decided I'm not looking back anymore—not with regret, not with bitterness. My past may explain me, but it does not define me. I'm choosing to move forward, not because it's easy, but because *I'm worth it.*

Forward means building a life of peace, joy, and impact. It means breaking generational curses so my children see what healing looks like. It means being the woman I once needed—and then some.

I'm no longer surviving. I'm creating. I'm leading. I'm walking in purpose. And I don't have all the answers, but I do have clarity: I know who I am. I know whose I am. And I know that everything I went through wasn't just for me—it was for someone else to be inspired to keep going.

So, here's what I want to leave with you—these life nuggets:

- **Don't be afraid to tell your truth.** Your story has power.
- **You can heal and still remember.** Memories don't disappear, but they lose their sting.
- **You are not alone.** Even in your darkest hour, there's still light ahead.
- **You are worthy.** Even if no one ever told you, you are enough.

This isn't the end of my story—it's just a new beginning. And I'm walking forward in faith, covered in grace, armed with forgiveness, and grounded in truth.

CHAPTER 9

PATHWAY POINTS
FAITH-FILLED INSIGHTS TO MOVE YOU FORWARD

1. Coming Home Doesn't Mean You Are Defeated
Returning home didn't make me weak—it reminded me of how much I'd grown. I came back stronger, with a clearer mind and a deeper understanding of who I was becoming.

2. Family Can Be Complicated and Still Be a Blessing
The relationships weren't perfect, but they were mine. Even in the dysfunction, I found connection, comfort, and moments of grace. I've learned to love people right where they are.

3. You Can't Change the Past, But You Can Grow From It
There were things I wish had been different—but instead of staying stuck in the "what-ifs," I chose to grow through the pain. Returning home gave me a new perspective on what healing looks like.

4. God Will Send You Back to Remind You What He Brought You Out Of
Sometimes God takes us full circle—not to break us down, but to show us how far we've come. I didn't realize it at the time, but my return was part of His refining process.

5. You Can't Heal What I Pretend Doesn't Hurt
Being back in that environment brought up feelings I had buried deep. But I've learned that facing those emotions is part of the healing journey. I don't have to pretend anymore—God can handle all of me.

Closing Note to the Reader

Dear Reader,

If you've made it to this point in my story, I want to pause and say thank you. *Thank you for walking with me through the cracks and crevices of my truth. Thank you for sitting with the pain, the process, and the progress. Thank you for holding space for a story that, at times, may have felt heavy—but I hope also felt healing.*

This book is more than just a memoir. It's a mirror—for the woman who's ever felt unseen, for the girl who had to grow up too fast, for the mother trying to get it right even when she feels she's falling apart, and for the soul who wonders if she's more than what life tried to label her.

You are.

I wrote this not to relive the past, but to redeem it. To declare that the cycles can stop with me. That scars don't disqualify us—they give us a story worth telling. That you can be both the wounded and the warrior, both healing and helping, both flawed and still chosen.

If there's anything I want you to walk away with, it's this:
You are not your pain.
You are not your past.
You are powerful, purposeful, and becoming more every day.

Your story matters. Your voice matters. You *matter. This isn't just about where I've been. It's about who I've become—and who* you *can become too.*

With love, faith, and forward movement,

Tinna Bellamy

*"My story isn't just about surviving —
it's about thriving, healing, and walking boldly
into the destiny God designed for me.
Faith carried me, forgiveness freed me,
and FORWARD is the only way I choose to go."*

TINNA BELLAMY

SERENITY PATHWAYS
FAITH FORGIVENESS & Moving FORWARD

TINNA BELLAMY

ABOUT THE AUTHOR

TINNA BELLAMY

ABOUT THE AUTHOR

TINNA BELLAMY

Tinna Bellamy is a woman of unshakable faith, purpose, and legacy. A devoted wife, mother, grandmother, and entrepreneur, she has transformed personal pain into purpose, using her life's challenges as steppingstones to inspire others. Tinna holds a master's degree in health administration and has built a thriving career in real estate. But her true calling lies in empowering others to break cycles, walk in healing, and step boldly into the future God has for them.

She is the founder of **Serenity Pathways Foundation**, a nonprofit organization dedicated to helping young adults—especially those aging out of foster care—establish stable, hope-filled lives. Through mentorship, education, and faith-based guidance, Tinna helps others discover that even broken beginnings can lead to beautiful destinies.

As the author of ***Serenity Pathways: Faith, Forgiveness and Moving Forward,*** Tinna shares her deeply personal journey of navigating abandonment, addiction in the home, and discovering her identity through God's love. Her story is one of resilience, redemption, and the unwavering belief that no matter where you start, God can take you further than you ever imagined.

TINNA BELLAMY

AUTHOR
SPEAKER
NONPROFIT FOUNDER

SERENITY
PATHWAYS
SERENITYPATHWAYSFOUNDATION.ORG

Book Tinna:

WEBSITE:
TINNABELLAMY.COM

EMAIL:
INFO@TINNABELLAMY.COM

Connect:

FACEBOOK: @TINNABELLAMY
TIKTOK: @TINNA.BELLAMY

Made in the USA
Columbia, SC
03 May 2025

57482625R00050